Everyday Life in
Victorian
Times

E. R. Chamberlin

MACDONALD YOUNG BOOKS

Contents

Introduction

The life of Queen Victoria spanned most of the 19th century. Born in 1819, she became Queen of England in 1837 and died, aged 82, in 1901. Her life was like a bridge connecting the past with the present, the old with the new. At the start of the century, life was not so very different from Roman times – although a Roman would have been rather shocked by the state of the roads and the filthy towns! But by the time of her death, life was not so very different from the world we know today.

In the early years the only way to travel on land was by foot or to use an animal. By 1901 steam trains were carrying millions of people at what seemed to be fantastic speeds (express trains went as fast as 150 kph). At sea, in 1805, the Battle of Trafalgar was fought by navies using sailing ships. These ships depended on the wind. If the wind stopped, the ship stopped. Sailors might even die of hunger while they waited for the wind to blow again. By 1901, iron and steel ships steamed the oceans, regardless of whether the wind blew or not.

People's lives changed just as much. In 1819 most people lived in country villages; by 1901 many of them lived and worked in towns. In the early years the food they ate came from the garden or a local farm. By the time Victoria died, it might have come from the other side of the world.

Inventors showered the world with new ideas – photography, gas lights, electric motors, gramophones, typewriters, and hundreds more. Today we take these inventions for granted: the Victorians were astonished by these 'marvels of science'.

The Great Exhibition

▶ The Medieval Court in the 1851 exhibition. This style of building and furniture was very popular in Victorian times, especially for churches.

In 1851 the world's first international exhibition was held in London. Called *The Great Exhibition of the Works of Industry of all Nations*, it was the brain-child of Prince Albert, Queen Victoria's husband. He was fascinated by science and industry and was proud of Britain's success. He wanted to show the world all the exciting new products streaming from Britain's factories.

The exhibition was held in the Crystal Palace, which was specially built in Hyde Park, London. The Crystal Palace was an example of new technology and building methods. Its cast iron frame held 300,000 panes of glass. The roof was so high that 30-metre elm trees grew inside it.

The exhibition was an enormous success. In twenty weeks six million people visited it. (At that time the population of London was less than three million.) Other countries rushed to copy the idea. Between 1851 and 1900 there were forty-one similar exhibitions in countries such as France, Germany, India, Australia and America.

A visitor to one of these exhibitions might see anything from a penknife with 80 blades, to a sewing machine, a giant steam engine or the latest huge cannon from the Krupps factory in Germany. All were examples of the latest technology.

▼ A wonder of science! Visitors marvelled at technical exhibits like this electric dynamo at the 1891 Frankfurt exhibition. Britain led the industrial world in 1851, but was soon rivalled by Germany and the USA.

▼ Britain's John Bull (far right) proudly leads the world to the Crystal Palace. Each person comes from a different country: for example, the man with a tuba is German. America's eagle leads the animals which include Britain's lion (arm-in-arm with the Prussian eagle and French cock) and the Russian bear.

12 February
1889

10 May
1888

9 September 1887

▲ New York's exhibition in 1858 copied the Crystal Palace design. It burnt down in a great fire. The English Crystal Palace was prefabricated (built from factory-made parts). After the exhibition it was taken apart and rebuilt 10 kilometres away. In 1936 it too burnt down.

▲ Each international exhibition tried to be bigger and better than the ones before. For the 1889 Paris exhibition, Gustave Eiffel built his famous tower to attract the crowds.

The Industrial Revolution

Around the time Queen Victoria was born, great changes were taking place in Britain. It was the time historians call 'the Industrial Revolution'.

It began with cloth. Cloth was made in different stages: wool or cotton fibres were cleaned, spun, dyed and, finally, woven into cloth. Workers in the cloth industry specialized in just one of these stages and worked from home. This made it difficult to control the quality and quantity of cloth. However, new machines were invented for these different stages. They were too big and expensive for people to buy and use in their homes, but they were ideal for use in a factory. Each factory with its machines could produce far more cloth than people working from home with simple tools.

The new factories meant unemployment for the traditional cloth-workers, but they also needed people to work the new machines. Most people in Britain still lived in the countryside and worked on the land. But, around this time, farmworkers' wages fell, while prices rose. So people flocked to work in the factories, little realizing how hard working in them would be. The factory workers needed somewhere to live, and towns grew up around the factories.

Eventually, industrialization spread to the rest of Europe. Belgium led the way with France and Germany

▲ This little girl worked in a cotton mill. Most workers in these factories were children or women. They had nimbler hands than men and could reach into the machines to clean them. Working conditions were terrible, and children often worked over twelve hours a day.

▼ An English coal pit-head in about 1820 with a steam winding engine. Without steam power, the Industrial Revolution could not have happened. By the 1780s James Watt had found a way to make the up-and-down motion of a steam piston drive a wheel. Steam engines drove the new factory machines.

following closely. By 1870, Germany rivalled Britain, and the USA produced more than all of Europe put together. But the spread of industrialization was patchy. Spain hardly changed at all, while in Italy the north became industrialized, but the south remained rural and poor.

▼ Forging the Shaft, *1877. This painting shows an American steel works, 75 kilometres north of New York. Despite new machinery and giant steam presses, heavy industry meant heavy work for the men. In the Krupps factories, (bottom) the men would have done similar work.*

▶ *The Krupp's armaments and steel works in Germany's Ruhr valley, 1870. By now regions like the Ruhr, northern France, Belgium, and northern England were dominated by factories and mills belching out filthy smoke from their chimneys. Compare how rapidly things had changed since the almost peaceful painting on the left, only fifty years earlier.*

Roads and canals

Travelling by road in the early 19th century was slow and uncomfortable. Most roads were stony, dusty tracks in summer and impassable bogs in winter. Engineers like Thomas Telford and John Macadam tackled the problem by building roads with firm foundations, good drainage and hard-wearing surfaces. Inns (called stages) along the new roads supplied fresh horses so people could travel rapidly on regular coach services at average speeds of 16 kph.

These new roads were expensive to build and maintain. One way of paying for them was to divide the roads into sections. Each section was run by a company which charged money (tolls) when travellers entered its section. However, this slowed down coaches and, by the 1850s, there were few toll roads left. Instead, roads were being built and paid for by governments using tax-payers' money.

Before railways came (Britain's first opened in 1825), water transport was the only way of moving heavy, bulky goods easily and cheaply. By the 1830s most European countries had networks of canals. The Scheldt canal linked eastern Belgium with the North Sea and, in 1840, a canal along the river Rhine joined Switzerland and Belgium.

Roads and canals were Europe's first efficient transport systems since Roman times. (Rome fell to invaders in 410 – 1400 years earlier!) But they were soon overtaken by the railways.

▲ *English locks. Barges going up hill entered the lowest lock. Water from the next lock was let into it until the barge floated up to the level of the next lock. By repeating this, the barge got to the top of the hill – in this case 18 metres above the lowest lock. It was a very slow system which took only one barge at a time. In the rest of Europe, new machinery, like the lift below, did the same job, but much more quickly.*

British canals could not compete with the railways. Today most are tourist attractions or in ruins.

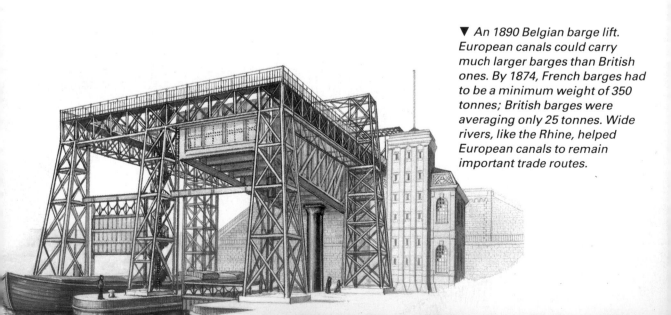

▼ *An 1890 Belgian barge lift. European canals could carry much larger barges than British ones. By 1874, French barges had to be a minimum weight of 350 tonnes; British barges were averaging only 25 tonnes. Wide rivers, like the Rhine, helped European canals to remain important trade routes.*

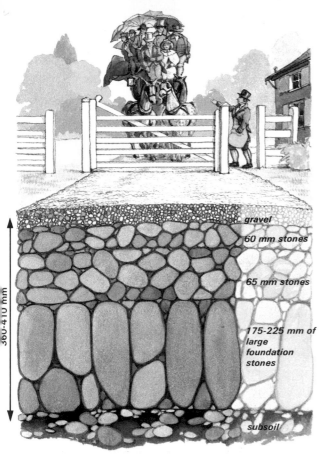

gravel
60 mm stones
65 mm stones
175-225 mm of large foundation stones
subsoil

360-410 mm

▲ Karl Benz, a German inventor, with one of the first motor cars. For many years a car was just a rich person's toy. In the 20th century cars eventually caused the decline of railways.

◄ A stage coach pays at a toll gate. Though stage coaches had a short life before the railways came, the British system was envied by Europeans for its speed. Young men often paid extra for the thrill of riding beside the driver. Beneath the road is a cross-section showing how Thomas Telford built his roads.

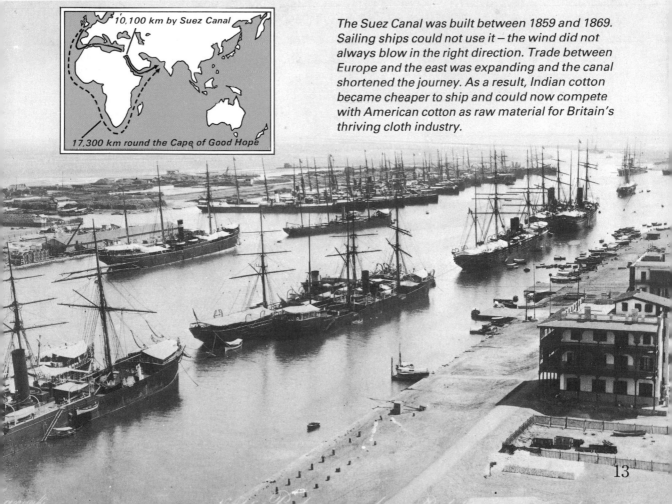

10,100 km by Suez Canal

17,300 km round the Cape of Good Hope

The Suez Canal was built between 1859 and 1869. Sailing ships could not use it – the wind did not always blow in the right direction. Trade between Europe and the east was expanding and the canal shortened the journey. As a result, Indian cotton became cheaper to ship and could now compete with American cotton as raw material for Britain's thriving cloth industry.

Ships and shipping

At the beginning of the period crossing the Atlantic took up to eight weeks. By 1901 it took about a week. The demand for shipping increased, too. People seeking new lives abroad, officials off to run the colonies, food for the growing populations of Europe and America and exports from Europe's factories, all needed ships.

Sailing ships were very efficient, so it was a long time before they were challenged by the new steam ships. The clipper *Cutty Sark*, for example, built in 1869, worked until the 1930s. Clippers (they 'clipped' time off voyages) raced valuable cargoes like Chinese tea and Australian wool to Europe and America.

In 1838 the *Sirius* won a race for the first steam ship to cross the Atlantic. Brunel's *Great Western* paddle steamer came second, losing by only three and a half hours, at an average speed of 16.3 kph. Early steam ships needed valuable cargo space to store coal and fresh water for the boilers. Their engines often blew up. But, by 1874, three-quarters of ships were steam-driven. Made of iron, and later of steel, steamships were not only stronger and faster than sailing ships, they could be much larger. As a result, shipping costs fell. In 1874 it cost twenty cents to ship a large sack of grain across the Atlantic. In 1904 it cost two cents.

▲ Britain had the world's largest merchant fleet; much of it was built in these Clyde shipyards. To protect the ships and keep shipping routes open, Britain also had the world's largest navy.

◄ Marseilles, France, about 1860. Increased international trade caused ports like Marseilles, New York, Hamburg, Rotterdam, Liverpool and Genoa to expand rapidly.

Wooden ships had a maximum size. Any bigger and they sagged in the middle. So, many more wooden ships than iron ships were needed to carry the same amount of cargo.

▲ *Brunel's* Great Eastern *being built in 1857, in London. At 17,160 tonnes, no bigger ship was built until 1901. It could carry 10,900 tonnes of coal and 4,000 passengers. Technically too far ahead of its time, the ship was a commercial failure.*

▼ *The* Great Eastern's *first-class saloon. Whether passengers went first-class or steerage (deep inside the ship, the worst and cheapest place), no-one could escape storms.*

Railways

No one person invented the railway. Instead, over many years, different ideas were combined until the railway emerged. The first *wooden* railways ran in mines so that horses could drag heavier waggons than on rough ground.

Early in the 19th century French and English engineers experimented with steam-powered road machines. Then, in 1813, George Stephenson designed and built a reliable 'locomotive' that could pull 30-tonne loads along iron rails.

The world's first public train steamed out of Darlington on September 27, 1825. From then, Britain's railways mushroomed: in 1843 there were 3,200 kilometres of tracks, by 1870 there were 22,000 kilometres. At first rich landowners feared the snorting iron dragons would terrify

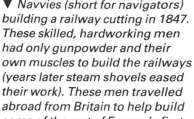

▼ *Navvies (short for navigators) building a railway cutting in 1847. These skilled, hardworking men had only gunpowder and their own muscles to build the railways (years later steam shovels eased their work). These men travelled abroad from Britain to help build some of the rest of Europe's first railways.*

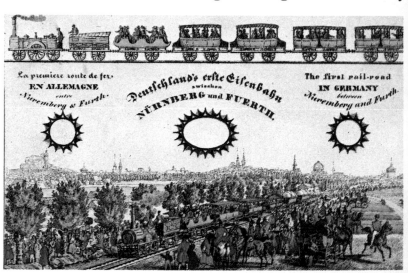

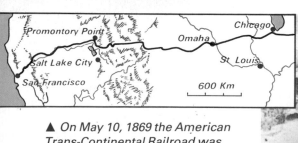

▲ *On May 10, 1869 the American Trans-Continental Railroad was opened. Two railroads, the Central, and the Union Pacific, started building lines from the west and east. They met at Promontory Point (right). The line opened up the vast American continent to thousands of settlers and farmers who could now send millions of cattle to the big cities and Europe.*

their cows and stop them giving milk. But when they realized the money to be made, they joined in the 'railway mania', scrambling to buy railway company shares or sell land for huge profits. Fortunes were made; but many were lost.

Continental railways developed more sensibly, mainly because they were longer and more expensive to build. In France and Italy lines were owned by the state and rented to private companies. German railways, too, got state aid. By the 1900s most European railways were state run: this did not happen in Britain until 1948.

▼ The railway terminus in Vienna, Austria's capital city. The photograph shows the outside, the painting the inside. Most railway companies were very successful. To show their success, many companies built huge, extravagantly decorated stations in the big cities. Some, like this one, or London's St Pancras station, looked more like medieval cathedrals than railway stations.

◄ The first German railway was opened in 1835 from Nuremburg to Fürth. Europe was quick to follow Britain's example; by 1850 the rest of Europe had 24,000 kilometres of railway tracks and by 1870, 104,000 kilometres of tracks.

Families

Parents were strict with their children. They loved them, but demanded respect and obedience in return. They hoped that family loyalties and a 'proper upbringing' would make their children become responsible and successful adults. Books like Mrs Isabella Beeton's *Book of Household Management* and an American book, *Fifteen Cent Dinners for Workingmen's Families*, were written to help people run their homes and families well.

Young children of rich parents were looked after by a nurse. They spent much of their time in a nursery where they could read colour picture books or the first pop-up books. *The Speaking Picturebook* even made the sound of an animal when a tab was pulled. Also in the nursery might be German clockwork trains, French china dolls or educational jigsaws. Governesses often gave children their first lessons at home. When he was old enough, a boy might join his father's business. His sisters helped at home, learning to become 'ladies' by practising the piano, embroidery or dancing, while waiting for 'suitable' husbands.

▼ *A very rich American family relaxes at home. Houses were large enough for grandparents to live in the same building. The children on the right are doing a jigsaw.*

◄ 'Street arabs' (poor children with no home). Hot air from a baker's oven came up through the grating they are sleeping on. This picture was taken in New York in the 1890s, but all cities had homeless children who had run away from cruel masters or whose parents had died.

The wives of wealthy men did not go out to work. Instead, they ran the household. It was a major task organizing the servants, but it was one of the few responsible jobs women had. Many also did 'charitable work' (helping the poor). Sometimes this led to work in local affairs. Slowly, women were becoming independent of men.

Poor people loved their children too, but it was much harder to look after a poor family. Many families who had worked together at home now worked in factories. Children might work in a different factory from their parents. Many children started working at five years old. Younger ones were often left with a minder. Many minders used 'infant preservatives' which contained drugs to make a child sleepy. But slowly, wages rose and many parents no longer had to force their children out to work. When working hours got shorter, people had more time to take children on outings or even holidays.

▼ A poor family at work in the 1890s. Goods like brushes, cigars or matchboxes, could not be made by machines. Instead, they were made by people working long hours at home for little pay.

Homes

Most people employed servants. Even a small home had a 'maid-of-all-work', who slept in the attic. A rich family might be outnumbered by its servants.

A humble servant's life was hard. She rose at 4.30 am and worked until 10.00 pm when she fell exhausted into bed. She probably only sat down to eat lunch or clean the silver cutlery. Coal was cheap, each room had a fire, so she spent much of her time heaving coal upstairs and ashes downstairs. Sunday was a 'rest' day when she got up half an hour later and went to bed half an hour earlier. Sometimes she had an afternoon off. For this, in 1860, she might earn £10 a year. However harsh, this life was still better than she could expect in the country, where most servants came from.

The factories produced so many cheap goods that people could afford things that used to be luxuries. Carpets and curtains, for example, were now found in quite ordinary homes. Gas lighting was used early in the period and eventually working people could afford it. Bathrooms were still a luxury for the poor who bathed in zinc tubs in front of the fire. Lavatories in poor areas were outside and often shared by over a hundred people.

Few people owned their houses; most rented them. Richer people paid every three months or once a year. Poorer people paid weekly. Anyone who fell behind with the rent was thrown out onto the street as the picture on page 35 shows.

▲ A servant in 1880 using the latest home labour-saving device – a mangle. Only the rich could afford washing machines and similar appliances.

▶ The drawing-room of a London house just as it was over eighty years ago. Linley Sambourne, the rich artist who lived here, drew the original black-and-white cartoons on pages 53 and 54.

▶ Many poor families, like this New York one in the 1880s, lived in just one room. As well as the four people here, a baby slept on a pile of old rags. Father heaved coal at the docks. 'When work was fairly brisk', he said, he earned about $5 a week.

▶ The cook (centre) with her 'slaveys' (maid servants) from a large house photographed in 1886. Male staff probably included a butler, gardeners and a coach driver. Even by Victorian standards this was a rich household. Servants got free board and lodging and some wages as well. A 14-year-old under-housemaid in 1884 earned about 20p a week – which would have bought a dozen eggs, a kilo of sausages and a kilo of cheese.

Fashion and clothes

A French postman

A British railway worker

▲ A new sight was civilian uniforms (military uniforms had been common for a long time). Thousands of people worked on the railways (900,000 in 1881 in Britain), in the police force or for the post office. Smart uniforms enabled everyone to recognize these people.

Early in the century men wore bright clothes. By the 1840s a well-dressed man's clothes were darker. A fashion book of the time insisted he should have four top-coats (a morning coat, a frock coat, a dress coat and an overcoat), seven pairs of trousers and five waistcoats!

Fine clothes showed how successful a person was. Hats indicated a man's class. Upper- and middle-class men wore top hats, working men might wear bowlers (known as 'billy-cocks'). Poor men made hats from old clothes or even folded them from paper. The very poor went bare-headed.

▼ These pictures show some of the changes in fashion between the beginning and the end of the period.

1860: A husband and wife off to the theatre. Men now wore shoes instead of boots and put macassar oil on their hair. The wife wears a crinoline over a tight corset. The maid wears an apron and cap.

1895: Women's suits had tight waists, often with a bustle (all that was left of the crinoline) behind. Sailor suits were popular for children, as were bloomers for sporty young women.

1800: Men still wore boots, but not fancy wigs. Women wore loose, flimsy 'empire' dresses more suitable for a hotter climate. At no other time in the century did women wear so little.

New factory-made dyes made women's clothes much brighter. Mauve was so popular that the 1890s were called the Mauve Decade. In 1862, an American, Amelia Bloomer, designed a trouser-like garment called 'bloomers'. Few women wore them until bicycling became popular.

Working people wore clothes similar to their grandparents. In the country farm workers still wore their traditional smocks. But cheap imported clothes from Germany allowed working people to be smarter on Sundays and holidays. Underclothes remained a luxury for the very poor.

▼ *Putting on a crinoline in five easy stages. Business boomed in the 1800s and it was mirrored in bigger and bigger skirts needing more and more petticoats to hold them up. By the mid 1850s, skirts were too heavy to wear, so crinolines were invented. Made of whalebone or springy steel, they stayed in fashion until the mid 1860s. No respectable woman showed her ankles. To avoid doing so, women often wore long pantaloons under crinolines. These pictures are from a set used in stereoscopes (page 42).*

◀ *A cotton mill. Wool was very expensive; cheap factory-made cotton allowed working people to dress better than ever before. Women's clothes often had bright, printed patterns.*

▼ *Clothes were never wasted. Children's clothes were handed down until they wore out. The poor bought dirty second-hand clothes at markets. Dirty clothes could spread diseases.*

Food and drink

▲ *Part of an advertisement for an 1897 oil stove. It cost £4.50, about twice as much as a labourer earned a week. The advertisement boasted that it could be run 'at one-third the cost of coal or gas', but it would have been expensive for poor people.*

Improved farming and cheap food imports gave people better and more varied food. From the 1870s onwards, refrigerated ships brought meat from Australia and America to Europe's ports. During the American Civil War (1861–65) H. J. Heinz started canning his '57 Varieties' for the two armies. Canning meant that food produced in one part of the world could be eaten much later elsewhere. Tea, coffee and cocoa fell in price, so helping reduce the amount of alcohol people drank. Sugar, once a luxury, was used to sweeten these drinks.

Not all food became better. Many poisonous substances were added to food to make it go further or look better. Red lead was added to cheese to colour it, acid to wine, chalk to flour and water to milk.

People still preferred meat and puddings to fresh vegetables and fruit. But they had more money to spend on food and were slowly becoming healthier. American tailors found that young men were a centimetre or so taller than their fathers.

In Britain dining-out and French food became fashionable. This was partly because many French chefs went abroad to escape the social unrest in France.

▶ *Many poor people could not afford a stove or coal to burn on it – they probably did not even have room for one. Often, there was no clean water for cooking. Instead, people took food to bakers who cooked it in their ovens.*

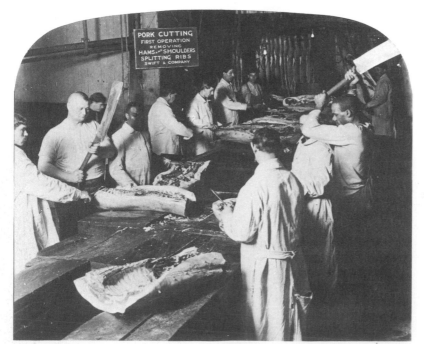

◀ *A Chicago meat factory. Like many other industries, much food production was done in factories. Not only could butchery be speeded up in a factory, but waste from carcasses – bones, skin, fat, and so on – could be used to make extra profits. This factory made 4,000 kilos of sausages a day and had 160,000 kilo vats for turning fat into soap. Most of the pigs and cattle reared in their millions on the great American plains went to Chicago for slaughter and packing.*

▲ Without railways, it would have been impossible to transport enough food to feed the people in the growing cities. So, without railways, cities could never have grown as big as they did.

▲ A hot potato seller. People worked long hours and might walk ten kilometres, or more, to work each day. They had little time or energy to cook meals. In busy city streets were people offering all sorts of things to eat: pies, lemonade, coffee, soup and many more.

► 'Buy my fresh milk, fresh, warm milk from the cow!' Milk goes bad so quickly that until there were fast refrigerated trains, dairy cows were kept in or very near the cities where their milk was sold.

25

Farming

Between the beginning and end of Queen Victoria's life Europe's population doubled to 400,000,000. Only a revolution in farming could feed everyone. Changes in farming had begun in England around 1700 and slowly spread to Europe and other parts of the world.

Farms produced more in different ways. Many poor farmers had split their farms between their sons so farms had become small and inefficient. In the 19th century many of these tiny farms were merged into bigger and more efficient ones. Farmers bred fatter, meatier animals, sheep with more wool, and cows which gave more milk. Old tools were improved and new ones introduced. Seed drills, for example, meant seeds were sown less wastefully.

By the 1870s cheap foreign food was flooding into Europe. European farming had to change to compete. Before this, most farms grew a bit of everything. By specializing, farms could produce much more, more cheaply. But more cheese, for example, was made than could be sold locally. The railways, however, could get the cheese to distant cities. Denmark and Holland changed from grain to dairy farming. Pigs and chickens are easy to keep on a dairy farm and by 1900 Denmark was selling eggs and bacon to Britain.

The farming revolution made many workers redundant. Food prices fell, so farmworkers were paid less. Rather than starve, millions left for town jobs or emigrated.

▲ The Flax Field *(Flax was used to make an expensive hard-wearing cloth called linen.) This Dutch painting of 1887 shows that, despite new machines, life for most farmworkers was hard, back-breaking labour. Women and children often did lighter tasks such as planting seedlings or picking crops.*

▶ *An Irish potato riot. In 1845 and 1846 potato blight caused widespread crop failures in parts of Europe. Irish peasants ate almost nothing but potatoes and could not afford any other food. Many died of starvation, while others emigrated to America. By the end of the century about 10,500,000 Irish had left their homeland.*

▲ At the top is a steam thresher in New Zealand. Steam ploughing was done with a stationary engine which dragged a plough on chains across a field. Most machinery, though, was still horse-drawn, like the American combine harvester below drawn by 33 horses photographed in 1887. Machines cut down the work in farming and, so, the cost of food.

▶ A cartoon of rich Russian landowners gambling with bundles of their serfs. Serfs worked on their owner's land and earned no wages. They could be sold with the owner's land – it was almost slavery. Russia finally abolished serfdom in 1861, though earlier in the century much of Europe, including Poland and Prussia, had serfs. Countries that kept serfdom the longest were often slow to industrialize.

Earning a living

The new industries and factories provided new ways to earn a living. Skilled men worked as engine-drivers, mechanics or electricians. But the Industrial Revolution also made life worse for millions of people.

In the past people had worked at their own pace in or near their homes. Now factory workers started and finished work at regular times, day in, day out, year in, year out. Machines stopped only for maintenance. Factory owners had to make the most of their expensive machines, so their workers had to work long hours. Fourteen hours a day was quite usual.

In factories children as young as five years minded machines. Children in mines were even worse off. Deep mines needed ventilation. So children sat in damp, lonely darkness opening and closing shutters to keep the air moving.

In England publicity about child sweeps caused an outrage. Before a child climbed the filthy, narrow chimneys, his master rubbed salt water into the boy's knees and elbows by a hot fire until the limbs bled. This treatment eventually hardened the skin. Reluctantly, governments in many countries abolished the worst of these abuses.

▲ An English coal pit-brow girl in 1867. Women usually did lighter work, but some did work as hard as the men's, shifting coal in, or above, the mines. Women did similar work in French and Belgian mines.

► Part of a painting called Work. Most middle- and upper-class Victorians believed that work improved you and was 'good for the soul'. The workers in this painting reflect this attitude with their handsome, noble and healthy faces. The reality was rather different as the Italian painting (far right) of a hatter shows. There was outrage when this painting was shown. People complained that it was too 'realistic'. They were especially angered by the man's dripping nose.

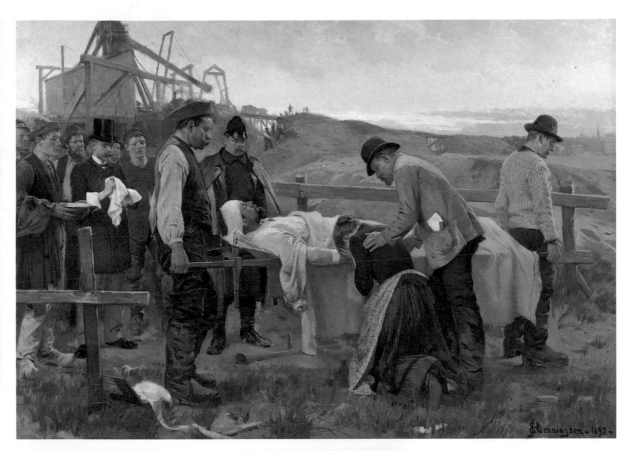

▲ The Wounded Workman *(a Swedish miner). Industrial accidents, diseases and deaths were horrifyingly common. Between 1856 and 1866 one thousand British miners died each year from accidents. For each recorded death there would have been even more unrecorded deaths from 'miners' lung' (caused by inhaling coal dust). Long before he died from it, a miner would have been sacked because he could not breathe well enough to do his job.*

Many machines had no guards on them to stop hands getting caught in the whirling machinery.

Few employers realized, or cared, that some of the materials their workers used were dangerous, such as phosphrous, which was used to make matches. The Mad Hatter in Alice in Wonderland *is based on hatters who used mercury to make hat felt. Mercury fumes damaged their brains.*

The growth of cities

In Europe at the beginning of the period there were 22 towns of more than 100,000 people. In America there were none. By 1901 there were 84 towns in Europe and 53 in America larger than this. Some cities now had over a million people. London was the largest (6,500,000), followed by Paris and Berlin.

Some ancient cities, like Lyons in France, grew with trade and industry. Many new cities developed through industry, but there were other causes. Chicago did not exist at all before 1800, but it grew fast because it was the central market for the meat, wheat and timber produced in the western USA. Oklahoma, also in the USA, grew overnight. Founded on 22 April 1889, by 23 April it had a population of 100,000, as settlers rushed in to claim land.

Land in city centres was expensive. Office buildings had to grow upwards. In 1891 New York had a steel-framed 21-storey skyscraper with an electric lift.

By 1851 more people in England lived in towns than the country. In Germany this happened by 1890 and in America not until 1920. Elsewhere, cities spread more slowly. In 1900 most Europeans were still country people. In France only 40% of the population lived in towns and in Scandinavia only 20%.

▶ By 1870 Chicago was a huge, busy city. But in 1820 it was just a few huts by a river (small picture below); it is the same river in both pictures. Chicago's growth was mainly due to the meat factories. Like many American cities, Chicago was neatly planned on a grid with streets running at right angles to each other.

▼ Sheffield in 1854 was Britain's major steel-producing city. Its population in 1801 was 46,000; by 1901 it was over eight times bigger. Like many other industrial cities, Sheffield grew rapidly with no attempts to plan its growth.

Overcrowding in Paris, 1886-1891

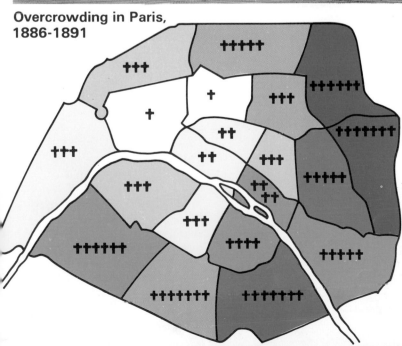

▼ This map shows the relationship between overcrowded living conditions and the number of deaths in the different districts of Paris. The least crowded (white) areas have fewest deaths. Any city could have had a map like this. As cities grew, more of the poor squeezed into old houses, causing more of them to die. By the 1870s, much of old Paris was rebuilt. Grand houses for the rich on wide streets (boulevards) replaced rotten slums. But nobody built new homes for the slum-dwellers forced out by the new buildings.

Numbers of deaths per 1,000 people each year.	
✝	14
✝✝	17
✝✝✝	20
✝✝✝✝	22
✝✝✝✝✝	25
✝✝✝✝✝✝	28
✝✝✝✝✝✝✝	31
% of people living more than two to a room.	
	5.5%
	8.0%
	10.7%
	13.4%
	16.1%
	18.7%
	21.4%

Life in the cities

Cities grew so big, so quickly, that it was almost impossible to provide essential things like clean water and sewers. London enlarged its sewers in the 1840s but still pumped waste into the river Thames. Filthy streets caused many outbreaks of disease, particularly cholera.

Pokey little houses were hurriedly and badly built for city workers. There were few building regulations and houses were often built back-to-back in narrow alleys with little sunlight or fresh air. Back rooms often had no windows.

So much coal was used for steam trains, factory engines and heating houses that cities were often under a permanent smoke cloud. Traditionally, rich and poor lived in the same areas, but late in the century many rich people moved to garden suburbs, away from the squalor of poor areas.

Many cities had parks or zoos, like London's Green Park or Berlin's *Tiergarten*. Other cities, like Paris, Vienna and Brussels, were less industrial and escaped the dense fogs that choked cities like London. Parisians enjoyed relaxing with a drink outside a café, something few Londoners would risk.

The invention of coal gas lights around 1800 meant that streets could be lit at night. So were the large department stores which were built from the 1840s onwards. Shopping arcades for the rich were built in every city. These were streets covered with glass on iron frames. Inside were shops selling all kinds of luxury goods away from the dirt of the street.

▲ This photograph was taken in Glasgow in 1868, but many of Europe's poor lived in similar overcrowded and unhealthy slums.

◄ Many parts of cities were badly lit and dangerous to walk in. Crime was common. This cartoon of 1856 makes fun of this (and the crinoline fashion!) by suggesting 'antigarrotting' (anti-strangling) clothing for men.

◀ A London traffic jam in 1872. Cities needed more and more horses to carry the people and goods that came in by railway each day. People walked or took horse-drawn cabs, buses or trams. The rich had private carriages. Freight went on horse-drawn waggons. London in the 1890s had 116,600 horses, which produced 400,000 tonnes of manure a year.

Towards the end of the century, city roads could no longer cope. The solution to the problem was to build railways inside cities. But there was no land left for new tracks, so in 1863 London built an underground steam railway. New York (below), Berlin and Düsseldorf built railways above the streets. By 1900, Paris, Vienna and other cities had begun building electric underground railways.

Crime and the misfits

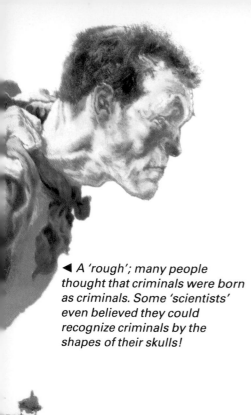

◀ A 'rough'; many people thought that criminals were born as criminals. Some 'scientists' even believed they could recognize criminals by the shapes of their skulls!

▼ Not only was it harder to control city crime than country crime, but there was more of it. British crime went up by eight times from 1805 to 1848. Crime rose when business slumped and jobs were scarce.

Factories made a few people wealthy, but they made millions more poor. Poverty was worst in the cities. Country people suffered harsh masters and famines – in an Italian famine peasants ate hay. But peasants could poach, gather firewood, or eat wild fruit; city people could not. If your work was not needed, you were instantly sacked. No social security helped the jobless, homeless or sick. Many people thought that the poor were poor through laziness.

Governments helped little and punished a lot. For example, British workhouses provided shelter for the poorest. But governments, terrified of encouraging 'idlers', made sure that people feared the workhouse and would do anything to keep out of it.

Most people lived honest lives, though some sank to amazing depths to get money – people even collected dogs' dung to sell to leather tanners. But some finally turned to crime. In 1829, to replace the army and night watchmen, Britain set up the world's first police force. Other European countries soon followed. Punishments were harsh. In Britain in 1800 hanging was the punishment for over 200 crimes. These included shoplifting, stealing bread, burning corn ricks and wrecking factory machines, because governments were worried that workers would revolt against the new factories.

◀ A Paris soup kitchen. Many poor and homeless starved or froze to death. Religious groups, like the French Sisters of Charity and the British Salvation Army, realized that being poor was not the fault of the poor and set up soup kitchens and cheap hostels. By the end of the century, such efforts made governments begin helping the poor.

▶ Evicted Tenants. *This Swedish painting of 1892 shows the fate awaiting people who could not pay their rent.*

Health and medicine

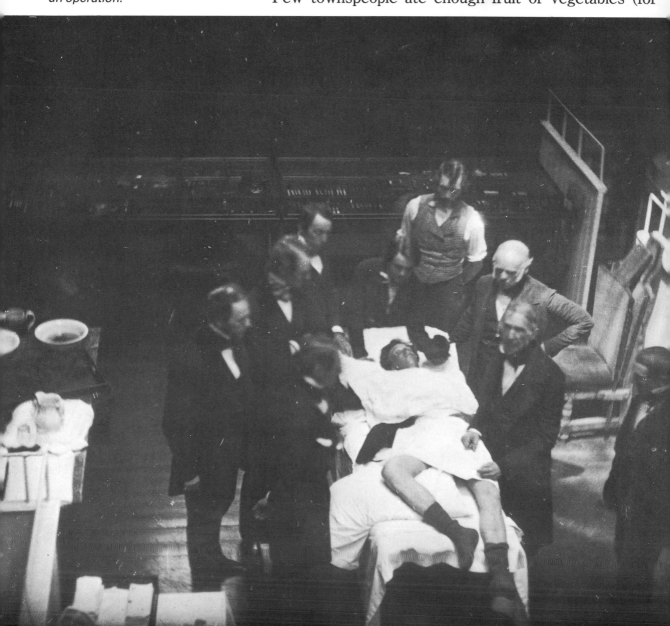

▼ An operation in America using anaesthetics (pain-killing drugs) in 1846. Before anaesthetics, patients were often made drunk so they would not notice the pain of an operation. Usually, if you had a leg sawn off, you died from shock and loss of blood rather than from what was wrong with your leg. Later, doctors like Joseph Lister in Scotland used antiseptics to stop people dying from gangrene (rotting flesh) after an operation.

In the 1830s cholera killed 100,000 French people. In 1849 it killed 16,000 Londoners. Cholera ravaged Europe. A London doctor realized that dirty water carried cholera, but most people ignored him. Then, in 1891, the disease hit Hamburg but not nearby Altona. Hamburg had dirty water, but Altona had special works to clean its water. The solution was clear: clean water defeated cholera.

Cramped, dirty cities bred killer diseases like cholera, smallpox, scarlet fever and typhus. Germ-laden water and festering rubbish attracted flies, whose next stop for food might be a baby's plate. Some people had to take turns to use a bed, so passing on their typhus-carrying fleas.

Few townspeople ate enough fruit or vegetables (for

vitamin C), so some got scurvy. Country people ate enough greenery (they could afford little else) to avoid it. Many children had bow legs from rickets, which is caused by too little sunshine and a poor diet.

In most families, at least one child died before its fifth birthday. But, slowly, life improved. Cheap soap and washable cotton clothes kept people cleaner. Water and sewage systems and housing improved gradually, and death rates began to fall.

Women had babies at home. One woman in four died giving birth. Families were large. The idea of contraception was a scandal and abortions were illegal. A woman exhausted by too many pregnancies could pay an illegal 'doctor' to carry out an abortion. The 'operation' was very dangerous and thousands of mothers as well as their babies died.

▼ Improved hygiene and better living conditions probably saved more lives than any medical advances. Efficient sewers were the most important improvements. These are sewers being laid in London in 1845. Paris got its first proper sewers when the city was rebuilt in the 1870s. Below the sewer picture is an angry cartoon published in 1828 showing 'monster soup' (London's filthy water) through a microscope.

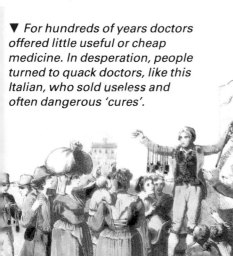

▼ For hundreds of years doctors offered little useful or cheap medicine. In desperation, people turned to quack doctors, like this Italian, who sold useless and often dangerous 'cures'.

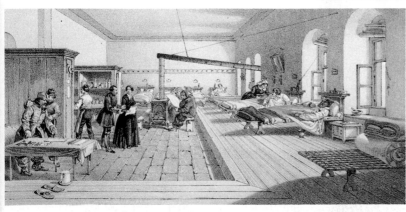

◄ Florence Nightingale was shocked at the state of the hospitals when she arrived in Turkey to look after British soldiers injured in the Crimean War. She cleaned up the rat-infested wards and made sure her patients were properly fed and looked after. She helped turn hospitals into places where people could expect to get better. She also made nursing one of the few respectable careers for educated women.

Communications

▼ In 1872 Eadweard Muybridge used 12 cameras to photograph this horse. Until then, galloping horses had been painted with their legs in impossible positions (like the horses on page 55). The first public movie show was held in 1895, 59 years after a Frenchman took the first still photograph.

In 1871, five minutes after the English Derby, the name of the winning horse was known 8,000 kilometres away in Calcutta, India. The electric telegraph sent news instantaneously. The *Great Eastern* laid the first trans-Atlantic cable in 1865 and by 1900 most of the world was cable-linked. Businessmen could instantly order new machines and governments could swiftly instruct distant colonies. The world was shrinking.

In the past the only way to send news had been to travel in person or send a messenger. In 1840 Britain started the first public postal service – the 'Penny Post'. For one penny a letter could be sent anywhere in the country. Other countries soon copied the idea.

'Mr Watson, come here, I want to see you.' These were the first words spoken on the telephone as Alexander Graham Bell talked to his assistant on his new invention on March 10 1876. British post office officials thought the idea would not catch on because there were plenty of messenger boys. They were soon proved wrong.

In 1812, in London, *The Times* became the first steam-printed newspaper. The machine was installed secretly to stop printers (who feared for their jobs) wrecking it. Later, automatic machines set type four times faster than hand-setters could. The New York *Daily Graphic* printed the first photograph (of New York slums) in 1880. After the 1830s cheap, popular newspapers challenged the dreary old papers. Books, too, became cheaper.

▲ Cheap printing made advertising easy, whether in magazines or posters in the street. This improvised advertisement hoarding is the wall of a derelict building. Yet another poster advertising a theatrical event is being pasted on to it.

◄ Magazines became so cheap that by the end of the century most people could afford them. The French and Italian papers below suggest that tastes then were similar to today's

◄ The first successful typewriter was sold in America in 1874. Busy businessmen found that educated women worked better than male clerks and for less money. Along with the telephone, the typewriter gave women another rare career opportunity.

Education

Throughout Europe the ruling classes believed that the poorer members of society should have the minimum of education. They feared that educated workers would revolt against them and the factory owners.

Many parents could not afford to send their children to school – it stopped them earning money. If poor children went to school it was to a church school. Church schooling was often bad. In 1850, for example, four out of ten young French army recruits could not read.

A few people thought that all children should have an education, not just the children of the rich. There was also a growing need for educated people to do new, skilled factory jobs. Schools began to teach 'useful' subjects – the '3Rs', *r*eading, w*r*iting, a*r*ithmetic.

Schooling slowly improved; but it was expensive and unpopular with voting tax-payers. Church leaders, especially in Catholic countries like France, Belgium and Italy, fought bitterly to keep control of education. But by the 1880s, in many European countries all children had to go to school, and there was free education for the poorest. Better education helped meet the demand for doctors, engineers and civil servants. By 1914, only one in ten young French soldiers could not read.

Girls' schooling was almost ignored until the end of the century when more thought was given to their needs. But even then it was often because governments realized that a man worked better if his wife fed him well and looked after his home and children. For example, German girls learned the '3Ks' – *Kinder, Küche, Kirche* (children, cooking, church).

▼ *A French church school, 1873. Often a poor child's only chance of education was to learn religion, morality and reading in a church or charity school. An English alphabet book began 'A stands for Angel, who praises the Lord; B stands for Bible, that teaches God's word.'*

► *Military-style P.E. exercises in 1888. Many pupils, especially city ones, had bad diets and were sickly and weak. Near the end of the century schools, led by those in Sweden, tried to improve children's health with games and exercises. In English schools for the sons of wealthy parents team games were meant to improve 'team spirit'. Elsewhere, team games were rare.*

► A London museum in 1840. Many people believed in 'self-help', or self-improvement. The growth of museums, public libraries and evening-classes let many working people overcome bad childhood schooling. It became easier to go to university as new colleges were set up.

► A Prussian school about 1880. Prussia (part of Germany) set the pace of junior education with state-run schools in the 1830s. German education tended to be practical and technical, providing ideas and skilled workers for Germany's growing chemical, electrical and optical industries.

German universities, like Bonn (1817), were based on France's École Polytechnique. But instead of producing army officers, they produced scientists or engineers.

Entertainment

▼ *In the evening a middle-class family might peer through a stereoscope which made two photographs magically appear in 3-D. If they tired of this, they might sing songs by the piano. Sheet music with bright covers was early pop music with hits like* The Great Exhibition Quadrille *or* Cook's Excursion Gallop *(which made fun of Thomas Cook's Italian excursion trips).*

'Scientific' toys gave well-to-do adults endless fun at home. Epidiascopes and magic lanterns projected flickering images onto walls. If you spun a Zoetrope (Wheel of Life) and looked through a slot, the pictures seemed to move. In 1895, the Lumière brothers astonished Paris with the first real movies, ten films lasting twenty minutes, twenty shows daily.

Most people could not such afford toys. They relaxed in bars, cafés or public houses. Others got drunk on poisonous brews in foul city drinking dens. In France and Britain, in particular, singers were used to attract custom. This led to music halls where entertainers included magicians, boxers, comics or strong-men. By the second half of the century, music hall stars were very popular with working people. London's Little Tich's silly dancing was famous across Europe. By 1890 Paris had become the pleasure capital of the world. This was largely due to entertainers like *La Goulou* (The Glutton), who danced the can-can in a swirl of lace to blaring trombones and crashing drums and cymbals, or Valentin (*Le Désossé*, the Boneless One), with his weird contortions.

There was plenty of street music, too. It could be an Italian organ grinder with a monkey, or the sad tin whistle of a crippled soldier. It might even be a splendid procession as the circus came to town. Circuses were very popular and many cities had permanent buildings for circuses.

▲ Many theatres were very
rowdy. People threw insults or
rotten fruit at artists they did not
like. Stage effects were often
astonishing: 'ghosts' appeared by
clever use of lights and mirrors;
real horses raced and naval
battles were fought with models
in giant water tanks.

▼ In the 1870s new sports, like
roller-skating, cycling and tennis
became popular with middle-
class people. Women joined in, so
gaining a little more freedom.
Watching professional football on
Saturday afternoons became
popular with British working men
after 1800.

▼ Drink was often called 'the
curse of the working class': many
people became ill or died through
alcohol. Men often spent their
wages on drink whilst their wives
and children went hungry. But
after a hard day's work it was hard
to relax in a dark, damp and
cramped slum room. Drinking
places, especially in Britain, were
often colourful and gave relief
from the misery of peoples' lives.

◄ The 'Greatest Show on Earth' –
Barnum and Bailey's circus –
comes to town! Its shows
included Tom Thumb and his wife
(both under one metre tall) and
the 'Original Stupendous Historic
and Spectacular Classic
Destruction of Rome'. A rival
'tenting' circus had a three-
kilometre procession with 70
horse-drawn waggons (20
carrying wild beasts), followed by
show horses and 100 Shetland
ponies. Elephants and camels
ambled along behind. It took nine
months to 'roll' over 3,000
kilometres, giving two shows a
day to 200 towns.

Highdays and holidays

Poor people worked long days with no paid holidays. Sunday was usually free and it might be the only day factory workers saw sunlight. Christmas and Easter were special holidays (though not as long as today) for all Christians. In Catholic countries saints' days were extra chances for rest days.

Most country towns had annual fairs where farmers sold or bought animals and their wives sold home-made cloth. Farm workers looked for next year's job and deals were agreed over a drink. To the scrapings of a beggar's fiddle, people munched spicey cakes or hot chestnuts, or tried catching a pig by its tail. Later, there was dancing far into the night.

Tourism was not new to the rich and it soon spread to the middle-classes. In 1864 Thomas Cook organized the first 'package tour' to Europe. His tourists read about the places they visited in new guidebooks published by a German, Karl Baedeker.

The poor could enjoy cheap excursions. In 1840 one train carried 3,000 people in 67 carriages drawn by four engines!

▲ Going for a country picnic on an 1862 cheap excursion bus. Before cheap buses and railways, working people's travel was limited by how far they could walk. It was difficult to get away from the city.

▶ Tourists watched this French Catholic festival in Brittany. For local peasants a saint's day was a chance to dress up in their best for the holiday. In Spain even the smallest town had a fiesta, when a town celebrated its saint's day with a holiday.

▼ Seaside holidays did not become popular until the last century when railways allowed townspeople to travel quickly and cheaply. This is Ramsgate in 1853.
 People were very modest and sunbathing was unheard of. If they bathed, they changed in bathing machines (huts on wheels, on the far right) into long-sleeved costumes covering most of their bodies. The bathing machines were wheeled into the sea until bathers could slip into the water unnoticed. When the children got bored with paddling, they could watch a Punch and Judy show (above the man playing the drum in the centre). The child with the spade is wearing pantaloons.

Religion

◀ This French painting, called Sunday, represents Heaven (the church) and Hell (the fiery furnace). It shows how church leaders hoped town workers would behave. Unfortunately, church leaders could no longer persuade people to go to church as regularly as they did in country villages. There were plenty of distractions in towns, like the inn in the lower left of the picture, to keep people away from church.

More realistically, some priests visited factories and mines to meet the workers. One German mine even had a tiny church for its workers.

▶ Many church leaders realized that they could no longer rely on people attending church. Instead, the church had to go out to meet the people. These Salvation Army officers are holding an open-air service in London's streets.

In Africa and other parts of the world European church missionaries tried to convert the native peoples to Christianity. Despite problems in Europe, Christianity was spreading throughout the world.

At the beginning of the period, most people lived in the country where the church was the centre of village life. Boys might go to a church school and families for many generations were baptized, married and buried at the same church. The church also usually helped the poor and the sick.

As people flocked to the towns, they lost touch with their country churches. Later, many large churches were built, often in poor parts of towns, to attract people back to God. Some organizations, like the French Sisters of Charity and the Salvation Army, felt that religion was not enough. They believed the poor needed food and shelter too. People like John Barnado set up homes for orphans in Britain.

Factory owners who treated their workers like tools and sacked them when they were no more use upset church leaders. But though they saw evil in the towns,

ideas of revolution alarmed churchmen even more.

In most Christian countries religion was in turmoil. Many educated people became uncertain about religion. They were not sure how much of the Bible they could really believe. At the beginning of Victoria's reign most people thought that the world was 6,000 years old. After the 1850s, however, scientists challenged such ideas and began a storm of argument.

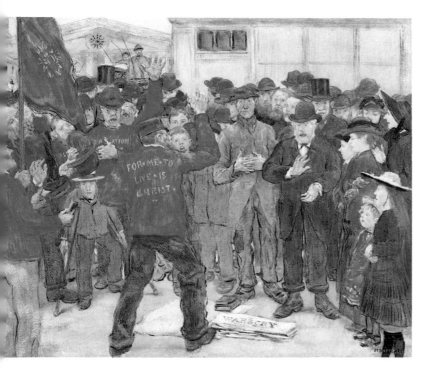

▼ A Russian Jew is hounded out of Kiev in 1881. Jews were viciously attacked in Eastern Europe.

Many Jews left Europe; in 1891 300,000 left Russia alone. The first Zionist congress in Switzerland in 1897 demanded a country in Palestine (now Israel) for all Jews where they could live in peace.

◀ A cartoon of Charles Darwin drawn in 1874. He believed all animals evolved (developed very slowly) from simpler animals. Human beings evolved from apes. This idea outraged church leaders – the Bible taught that God created every animal 'ready-made' in six days. Geologists realized that rocks contained fossil remains of extinct animals, whilst others showed that the earth's rocks were millions of years older than the Bible claimed. In Vienna Sigmund Freud shocked people with his ideas about human behaviour. All these scientists undermined the teachings of churches.

Warfare

Machines revolutionized wars. Some generals no longer even led their troops into battle. The brilliant German general Helmuth von Moltke (1800–91) commanded his troops by telegraph from his Berlin desk. Armies were now so big that only railways could move the thousands of men and their supplies.

Old rifles were muzzle-loaded. A soldier stood up and rammed the ball and powder down the barrel with a long rod. The guns were inaccurate and three shots a minute was a fast rate of fire. New breech-rifles were loaded in a slot in the barrel by the handle. A soldier could do this lying down in safety. Breech rifles also fired further and more rapidly. In 1862 Dr Gatling invented a machine gun which fired 700 shots a minute. As American Civil War soldiers discovered, one man armed with a machine gun could mow down hundreds of people.

In the same war, the warships *Merrimac* and *Monitor* fought the first 'ironclad' duel. The wooden sailing ship, at the wind's mercy, was on its way out. Like the new guns used by soldiers on land, ships' guns were also improved, becoming more accurate and deadly.

In 1859 39,000 men were killed or injured at the Battle of Solferino. Horrified by this slaughter, Jean Dunant, a wealthy Swiss man, founded the Red Cross in 1864. It still cares for people wounded and captured in any war anywhere. Attempts to stop the international arms race in the 1890s were not so successful, but deadly poison gas, at least, was banned.

▲ *Balloons were sometimes used to spy on enemy troops. This one was used during the siege of Paris during the Franco-Prussian War (1870–71). It flew messages out of the city.*

▼ *War, like all other aspects of life, was affected by the Industrial Revolution. Nowhere was this more obvious than at sea. At the start of the century fighting ships were wooden sailing ships that had hardly changed in centuries. By 1901 they were steam-driven monsters with thick steel armour and guns which could hurl huge shells over 18 kilometres. In the middle of the century, these two extremes overlapped in ships like La Gloire.*

Constitution (USA, 1797)

A fast ship, but smaller than Britain's huge ships like the Victory, *which used about 2,000 oak trees to build it.*

La Gloire (France, 1859)

The first ship with iron armour on a wooden hull. Britain, not wanting to be outclassed, built the first all iron warship in 1860.

▲ Dead Americans on a Civil War battlefield. Most people thought war was a 'glorious thing'. To join a fashionable brigade was the ambition of many young men. Most battle paintings helped this belief, and they rarely showed the true picture. War photographs may have helped show people the shocking reality of war.

▶ Above all else, railways revolutionized land warfare. Wars speeded up because, instead of long, tiring marches, foot troops arrived quickly, fresh for battle. Germany first used railways successfully. Without railways, the huge armies of World War One could not have moved.

Potemkin (Russia, 1900)

▼ An 1879 steam submarine. A submarine sank an enemy ship in 1863 in the American Civil War – unfortunately, it sank itself at the same time! Submarines were not yet practical, but by 1914 they were ready to sink hundreds of ships.

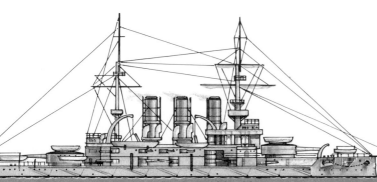

A typical battleship of the time with 130 mm thick steel armour. As well as guns, it had four torpedo tubes.

Revolutionaries

In the 1830s France, Belgium, Poland, Switzerland and parts of Germany and Italy were in revolt. In 1848 and 1849 there were revolutions throughout Europe.

More people could read; cheap newspapers told them what their rulers were up to. Townspeople could easily go to meetings where fiery speakers could arouse thousands to anger. Then it was easy to form a mob.

Some revolutionaries were educated idealists, others were poor workers. Many were nationalists who hated foreign rulers. Often all these people joined together in revolt. It was confusing: rich and poor together fought foreigners, while poor people might fight against their own rulers. This lack of unity caused most revolutions to fail. But the revolutions frightened the rulers. Gradually, they were forced to take more notice of people's demands.

German and British workers began cooperative societies to buy things more cheaply from factories. Most Danish butter, eggs, cheese and bacon were produced cooperatively. Belgian co-ops ran shops, cafés and libraries. By 1890 trade unions were legal in most countries. The first unions helped skilled workers in sickness or death; they rarely struck for more pay. But in the 1880s and 1890s unions of less skilled workers struggled for more pay. French foresters, German miners and British match girls and dockers all fought bitter strikes. Working people were gaining strength to fight their employers for better pay and working conditions.

▲ Karl Marx is the most important person in socialism's history. Helped by his friend, Friedrich Engels, he wrote pamphlets and books about industrial countries. He thought that working people were exploited and that the only way to stop this was for workers to seize power from their rulers. He wanted to see 'working men of all countries unite', for they had 'nothing to lose but their chains'. Marx said revolution would begin in the most industrial country – Britain. Instead, it was in backward Russia that peasants made the first successful socialist revolution in 1917.

▶ The last great Chartist meeting in 1848. Chartism was an idealistic British movement whose aims included votes for all men and annual general elections. It included intellectuals, workers who hated the factories and hand-loom weavers whose jobs were threatened by the factories.

Some meetings were broken up by the army. But, in general, British people had a little more freedom than most Europeans. It was enough to prevent a British revolution in 1848.

◄ This French cartoon is ironically called Liberty. A fat, bloated capitalist (a factory owner and employer of workers), protected by soldiers, watches down-trodden workers trudge to work in his factory. Cartoons like this were meant to anger people into revolt.

▼ A street barricade in the Paris Commune (1871). After France's defeat in the Franco-Prussian war, thousands of Parisians felt betrayed by their government and revolted against it. For six weeks they held the city with barricaded roads. Government troops defeated them and killed or executed 30,000 of the rebels. The Commune inspired revolutionaries to believe that a successful revolution was not far away.

► London dockers in 1871 protest against the treatment of fellow workers in the unsuccessful Paris Commune revolt. Many workers believed their loyalties should be with other workers and not with bosses, church leaders or politicians. Improved communications and newspapers encouraged this feeling.

Nations old and new

People always feel drawn towards people who speak the same language and have similar customs. This is called nationalism.

At the beginning of the Victorian era many Europeans felt threatened by outsiders or were ruled by foreigners. Slowly, they began to ask themselves 'Why?' For example, in 1800 there was no such country as Italy. But people were beginning to see themselves as *Italians*, not Venetians, Romans or Neapolitans. After many struggles, when Italians fought Italians and Italians fought foreigners, Italy finally became a united country in 1871. Germany did not exist in 1800, either. But, led by Prussia, which had defeated Denmark, Austria and France, the 38 kingdoms and states were united into one country in 1871.

Elsewhere, nationalist feelings were stifled and this

▼ *Most European royal families were related to each other by birth or marriage. Queen Victoria was mother, grandmother or great grandmother to most of them. Victoria's grandchildren included the Czarina of Russia, the Queens of Romania and Norway, and Kaiser Wilhelm II. Here is Victoria (1) with more of her family: Princess Marie Louise of Schleswig-Holstein (2); Princess Margaret, later Crown Princess of Sweden (3); the Duke of York, later Britain's King George V (4); Prince Albert of York, later Britain's King George VI (5); Princess Victoria Eugenie, later Queen of Spain (6).*

▶ *Queen Victoria ruled Britain from 1837 to 1901. She became a symbol of the power and wealth of Britain and her empire. In her old age, people would drink a solemn Christmas toast to 'the dear old Queen'. Her Diamond Jubilee (60 years on the throne) was joyously celebrated – even the very poor were given free banquets. This photograph shows a shooting stall. Prizes included Jubilee mugs and plates with the Queen's portrait on them.*

meant trouble. In the huge Turkish Empire, Muslims and Christians could not get on with each other. Greece and Romania broke away and the empire became so rickety that it was called 'the Sick Man of Europe'. The Austro-Hungarian Empire was made up of a hotchpotch of nationalities including Poles, Slovaks, Italians, Hungarians and Czechs, all speaking different languages. Nationalist revolts constantly threatened the empire and parts of it broke away. Somehow, it survived. But nationalism is a very powerful force. Eventually it destroyed the empire and devastated Europe in World War One (1914–18).

▼ Franz-Josef (the policeman in this 1878 cartoon), ruler of the Austro-Hungarian Empire, tries to control two of his countries (the unruly children, Bosnia and Herzogovina). The empire included many different peoples who demanded their freedom from his hated rule. In 1914 Franz-Josef's nephew was murdered in Bosnia by the man being arrested in the photograph. World War One began as a result.

◄ Loyal, enthusiastic Prussians loudly cheer their king, Wilhelm, as he leaves Berlin to join his army in the war against France in 1870.

Five months later France surrendered and Germany became one nation. Prussia was the biggest and most powerful of the German kingdoms, so Wilhelm became Kaiser (Emperor) Wilhelm I of Germany.

53

European empires

Many European countries built up huge empires during the Victorian period. By 1902 they owned over 70% of the world. Belgium had a vast empire (80 times its own size) in the Congo in central Africa. King Leopold ran it as if it were his own personal property. Britain's empire was the largest of all: 345,000,000 people and 28,000,000 square kilometres.

Empire building speeded up in the 1870s and 1880s for many reasons. Missionaries, off to convert native peoples to Christianity, usually arrived first. Traders in goods like gold, fur or diamonds followed them. Many Dutch, French and British colonies were started and run by companies like the East India Company which ruled India until 1858.

European countries sold the goods their factories made in their empires. Britain earned the then enormous sum of £8,000,000 a year from her empire (apart from India). But it cost £4,000,000 to run it and even more fighting to

▲ Cecil Rhodes astride Africa. He dreamed of a railway, as well as the telegraph line he holds, linking north and south Africa from Cairo to the Cape. Rhodes helped Britain claim much of Africa. He once said he would colonize the planets if he could.

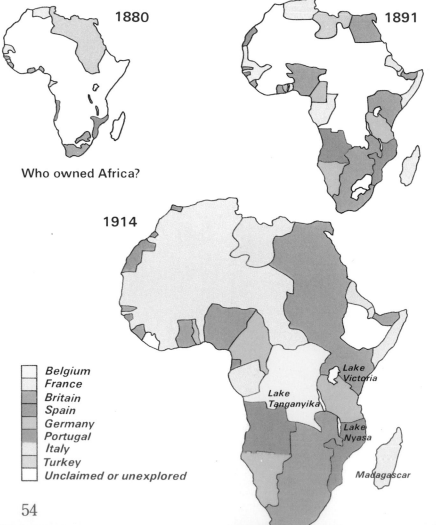

1880

1891

Who owned Africa?

1914

- Belgium
- France
- Britain
- Spain
- Germany
- Portugal
- Italy
- Turkey
- Unclaimed or unexplored

Lake Victoria

Lake Tanganyika

Lake Nyasa

Madagascar

◀ For over half the century much of Africa was unexplored. But by 1880 a European 'scramble for Africa' had begun. These maps show what happened.

During the century Europeans extended their control of the rest of the world. Europe had ruled many countries earlier; Spain and Portugal had had huge South American empires but had lost most of them by 1830. Most of India was British-run by 1800 and in the Far East, the Dutch and British had great power, while the French ruled Vietnam.

Many European countries took whatever land they could, even if it was useless. Often, it was just to stop others taking it first.

defend it. To help British ships on their long trading journeys, Britain used places like the Falkland Isles and Malta to refuel the ships with coal and food.

Steamships could rush troops to crush native revolts with their superior weapons. News of such 'heroic' deeds aroused nationalist pride in European voters. Even if governments could not really afford empires, they were popular with their people. Hardly anyone thought about the people whose land was being taken.

▼ African police wearing uniforms more suitable for European climates than for Africa. Europeans who ruled a country took their customs with them. Today Spanish is spoken where Spain once ruled, and where France ruled, you can still enjoy French cooking.

Native people employed by Europeans were poorly paid and badly treated. Belgian Congo Africans were treated like slaves.

▼ Settlers chase Australian aborigines off the land. Tribes suffered if they did not fit in with white settlers' plans for the land. Tasmanian aborigines were wiped out. Much of the USA was stolen from the Indians and thousands of them were killed. Sixty million bison, which the Indians used for food, clothing, tools and tents, were shot by settlers. If these tactics failed, native peoples often died of diseases brought by the settlers.

New lives in new lands

▼ *Steerage class for trans-Atlantic emigrants. It was described in 1847 as 'hundreds of poor people, men, women, and children, of all ages, from the drivelling idiot of ninety to the babe just born, huddled together, without light, without air, wallowing in filth and breathing a (foul) atmosphere, sick in body, dispirited in heart'. Food was bad, and in short supply; you took your own if you had money.*

Steam ships cut crossings to ten days. But steam travel was far too expensive for most emigrants.

In 1850 a tired farm worker relaxed at an inn. On the wall, a poster described 'ships of the largest class commanded by men of experience, who will take every precaution to promote the health and comfort of passengers' on the voyage. He had heard tales of free farmland in America. He needed £3.50 for the fare and as much again for food and clothes on the trip. His weekly wage was 35p. Once there, he could send tickets for his wife and children to follow him out to his new farm. Nobody would be his boss and he might even buy a horse and carriage . . .

Many a new life abroad began like this. The population of Europe increased by 210,000,000 during Queen Victoria's lifetime. There were not enough jobs, homes or food for everyone. Until the 1880s it was mainly Irish,

▶ *Newly arrived Scandinavians wait at New York's landing station. Many immigrants came from very poor countries. New York, was a flashy, busy city. You could read long lists of New Yorkers worth $100,000 or more. Richest of all was J. J. Astor, who was once a poor immigrant himself. He had a fortune of $25,000,000. New immigrants dreamed of his sort of success. Instead, crooks often conned the ignorant peasants out of their tiny savings as they landed.*

Britons and Germans who risked the four to eight week long Atlantic crossing. Few ships had doctors and many passengers died. One ship left Liverpool with 634 emigrants, but only 476 reached New York. After 1870, 21,000,000 Poles, Greeks, Hungarians, Italians and Jews left Europe, half for the USA, the rest for New Zealand, Australia, Canada, South America or South Africa. Many, especially Jews, left Europe to escape persecution.

On New York's Statue of Liberty (a gift from France in 1886) are the words 'Give me your tired, your poor, your huddled masses, yearning to breathe free'. But some Americans were worried by the floods of foreigners pouring into their country. They felt they were a threat. Fears like this stopped Chinese emigrants after 1882.

◀ Australian gold fever in the 1850s. Life was so grim for many Europeans, that only dreams of a new life kept them going. Newspaper reports of gold finds in South Africa, the USA and Australia always produced extra rushes of hopeful immigrants. Few made their fortunes.

At first Australia was a dumping ground for British convicts. Few people were prepared to face the 13,000 kilometre sea trip. Steam ships, gold and news of rich farmland changed all that.

▶ A settlers' waggon train heads west across the Rockies. Many immigrants dreamed of a land of 'milk and honey' that was there for the taking in the Wild West. Most of the 29,500,000 Italians, Irish, Germans and British who arrived in eastern America could not afford the trek out west. Instead, they ended up working in the booming factories.

Main events

1801 United Kingdom formed by union of Great Britain and Northern Ireland.

1802 *Charlotte Dundas*, the first steamship, sails on the river Clyde in Scotland.

1804 Napoleon Bonaparte crowns himself emperor of the French.
First experimental steam locomotive runs on rails in England.

1805 Battle of Trafalgar won by Britain over France.

1807 Slavery abolished in British Empire.

1812 Napoleon invades Russia

1814 Napoleon abdicates from throne.

1815 Battle of Waterloo.
Napoleon exiled to St Helena.

1816 Argentina wins freedom from Spain.

1819 Birth of Queen Victoria.
'Macadam' roads laid in Britain.

1821 The Greek War of Independence against Turkey begins.

1823 'Monroe Doctrine' announced by USA; Europe told not to interfere in South America.
'Macintosh' – waterproof material – invented by Charles Macintosh.

1824 Beethoven finishes ninth symphony.

1825 Erie Canal links New York with the Great Lakes, 520 km away.

1830 Charles X, the King of France, deposed.

1832 Electric telegraph invented.
Greece becomes independent of Turkey.

1835 The 'Great Trek' of the Boers begins in South Africa.

1837 Victoria becomes Queen of Britain.

1840 Antarctic coast discovered.
Rowland Hill starts 'Penny Post'.

1845 Submarine telegraph cable laid between France and England.
Potato famine begins in Ireland.

1847 Chloroform used successfully as an anaesthetic for the first time.

1848 The 'Year of Revolutions': France, Austria, Italy, Croatia, Germany and Sicily all have revolts.
Gold rush in California.
First settlers in New Zealand.
Marx publishes *Communist Manifesto*.

1849 David Livingstone begins exploration in Africa.

1851 Gold rush in Australia.
Great Exhibition opens in London.

1854 America opens up Japan to trade with the rest of the world.

1854 Crimean War between Russia and the Allies (France, Britain, Turkey and Sardinia).

1855 Florence Nightingale begins hospital reform in Scutari, Turkey.

1856 Henry Bessemer invents a way to make steel cheaply from iron.

1857 Indian Mutiny.

1858 First trans-Atlantic telegraph cable laid.

1859 Darwin publishes *Origin of Species*.
Petroleum found in Pennsylvania, USA; used for heating and lighting.

1861 Serfs in Russia given their freedom.
American Civil War begins.

1863 First underground railway in London.

1864 War between Denmark and Prussia.
International Red Cross founded.

1865 American Civil War ends. Lincoln, president of USA, assassinated.

1867 Alfred Nobel invents dynamite; later founds Nobel Prizes for peace, physics, chemistry, medicine and literature.
USA buys Alaska for $7,200,000 from Russia.

1869 Suez Canal opens.
Transcontinental Railroad completed in USA.

1870 The Pope declares himself 'infallible', meaning he can make no mistakes about morals or faith.

1871 Zanzibar slave market closed through British pressure. Italy unified. German Empire founded. Paris Commune set up, but fails later.	# Famous People

1871 Zanzibar slave market closed through British pressure.
Italy unified.
German Empire founded.
Paris Commune set up, but fails later.

1874 Factory Act in Britain limits hours of work.
Typewriter invented.

1875 Britain buys Egyptian share of Suez Canal so increasing control over it.

1876 First railway in China.
Telephone invented.
First motor car runs.

1877 First frozen meat cargo arrives in Britain from Argentina.
Edison patents cylinder phonograph (early gramophone).

1880 Cause of malaria discovered.

1881 Pasteur successfully immunizes people against anthrax.
Czar Alexander II of Russia assassinated.

1884 Rules for taking over Africa drawn up by European countries in Berlin.
Automatic rifle invented by Maxim.

1885 National Congress formed in India as first step to independence.

1888 Pneumatic tyre invented by Dunlop.
Greenland ice-cap crossed.

1889 Eiffel Tower built.

1891 Trans-Siberian railway begun.

1893 Britain acquires Uganda.

1894 Moving pictures (cinematograph) invented by Lumiére brothers.

1895 X-rays discovered.
Kiel canal opened in Germany.

1896 Marconi invents wireless telegraphy.

1897 Queen Victoria's Diamond Jubilee.

1898 Pierre and Marie Curie discover the effects of radium.
Spanish-American War: USA acquires Phillipine Islands.

1899 Boer War begins.

1901 Death of Queen Victoria.

Famous People

Prince Albert (1819–61) was Queen Victoria's beloved German husband. His death from typhoid devastated her.

Phineas T. Barnum (1810–91) was a brash American showman famous for his shows and circuses.

Isabella Beeton (1833–65) wrote cookery books that sold 2,000,000 copies in the first ten years.

Amelia Bloomer (1828–94) was an American who fought for women's rights, despite people's ridicule.

Isambard Kingdom Brunel (1806–59), a British engineer, built ships, tunnels, bridges and railways.

Gustave Eiffel (1832–1923), a French engineer, famous for the Eiffel Tower.

Sigmund Freud (1856–1939), an Austrian, who began the scientific study of human behaviour.

Baron Haussman (1809–91) demolished much of old Paris and rebuilt it with wide streets difficult to barricade.

Alfred Krupp (1812–1887) turned a small iron works into Germany's giant Ruhr steel and armaments factories.

Joseph Lister (1827–1912) discovered that carbolic acid kills germs.

Helmuth von Moltke (1800–91), a Prussian military genius, who crushed Austria-Hungary and France.

Florence Nightingale (1820–1910) fought to become a nurse. She brilliantly reorganized the Crimean hospitals.

Louis Pasteur (1822–95) made the major discovery of how germs are passed on.

George Stephenson (1781–1848) built the first reliable steam locomotive for a public railway.

James Watt (1736–1819), a Scot who greatly improved the steam engine.

Glossary

American Civil War (1861–65) It was fought between 11 Southern states (which wanted to break away from the USA) and the Northern states. One cause was slavery: the South wanted it, the North did not. A million people died before the South was defeated.

Austro-Hungarian Empire The ancient Habsburg empire once ruled much of Europe. By 1867 its Viennese rulers were losing control of the empire: they agreed to share power with the Hungarians. The empire was then called the Austro-Hungarian Empire. Besides Austria and Hungary, it included parts of today's Italy, Yugoslavia, Czechoslovakia, Poland and Romania.

emigrants People who leave one country to live in another.

Franco-Prussian War (1870–71) France and Prussia were rivals, and this led to war. The Prussians won.

immigrants People living in one country who were born in another.

middle-class People not so rich as the upper-class. Most were well educated. They included army and navy officers, vicars and priests, teachers and businessmen.

upper- and **ruling-classes** The richest and most powerful people who controlled, or ruled, people's lives. They included kings or queens, politicians, bishops, rich businessmen and army and navy commanders.

Victorians Queen Victoria ruled Britain for so much of the century, that 19th-century people are often called Victorians.

working-class This was the biggest class of people. They were poor and usually lived in the worst parts of cities. They were often badly educated. They included farm and factory workers, servants, shopworkers and ordinary sailors and soldiers.

Index